MAURICE SENDAK

A Real-Life Reader Biography

Ann Gaines

Mitchell Lane Publishers, Inc.

P.O. Box 619
Bear, Delaware 19701

Mitchell Lane PUBLISHERS

First Printing

Real-Life Reader Biographies

Paula Abdul	Mary Joe Fernandez	Ricky Martin	Arnold Schwarzenegger
Christina Aguilera	Andres Galarraga	Mark McGwire	Selena
Marc Anthony	Sarah Michelle Gellar	Alyssa Milano	**Maurice Sendak**
Drew Barrymore	Jeff Gordon	Mandy Moore	Dr. Seuss
Brandy	Mia Hamm	Chuck Norris	Shakira
Garth Brooks	Melissa Joan Hart	Tommy Nuñez	Alicia Silverstone
Kobe Bryant	Jennifer Love Hewitt	Rosie O'Donnell	Jessica Simpson
Sandra Bullock	Faith Hill	Rafael Palmeiro	Sinbad
Mariah Carey	Hollywood Hogan	Gary Paulsen	Jimmy Smits
Cesar Chavez	Katie Holmes	Freddie Prinze, Jr.	Sammy Sosa
Christopher Paul Curtis	Enrique Iglesias	Julia Roberts	Britney Spears
Roald Dahl	Derek Jeter	Robert Rodriguez	Sheryl Swoopes
Oscar De La Hoya	Steve Jobs	J.K. Rowling	Shania Twain
Trent Dimas	Michelle Kwan	Keri Russell	Liv Tyler
Celine Dion	Bruce Lee	Winona Ryder	Robin Williams
Sheila E.	Jennifer Lopez	Cristina Saralegui	Vanessa Williams
Gloria Estefan	Cheech Marin		Tiger Woods

Library of Congress Cataloging-in-Publication Data
Gaines, Ann.
    Maurice Sendak/Ann Gaines.
        p. cm.—(A real-life reader biography)
    Includes index.
    ISBN 1-58415-079-3
    1. Sendak, Maurice—Juvenile literature. 2. Authors, American—20th century—Biography—Juvenile literature. 3. Illustrators—United States—Biography—Juvenile literature. 4. Children's stories—Authorship—Juvenile literature [1. Sendak, Maurice. 2. Authors, American. 3. Illustrators.] I Title. II. Series.
PS3569.E6 Z68 2001
741.6'42'092—dc21
[B]
                                                  2001029452

ABOUT THE AUTHOR: Ann Graham Gaines holds graduate degrees in American Civilization and Library and Information Science from the University of Texas at Austin. She has been a freelance writer for 18 years, specializing in nonfiction for children. She lives near Gonzales, Texas with her husband and their four children.

PHOTO CREDITS: cover: Archive Photos/Armen Kachaturian; p. 4 Stephen Castagneio/New York Times; p. 6 Archive Photos; p. 21 Sam Falk/New York Times; p. 25 Globe Photos; p. 28 Rick Wilking/Archive Photos.

ACKNOWLEDGMENTS: The following story has been thoroughly researched, and to the best of our knowledge, represents a true story. While every possible effort has been made to ensure accuracy, the publisher will not assume liability for damages caused by inaccuracies in the data, and makes no warranty on the accuracy of the information contained herein. This story has not been authorized nor endorsed by Maurice Sendak.

Table of Contents

Chapter 1
Where the Wild Things Are

Many grown-ups did not like author and illustrator Maurice Sendak's first picture book, *Where the Wild Things Are*, which was published in 1963. In this book, a small boy named Max makes his mother furious. Wearing his wolf costume, he's chasing the family dog and getting into all kinds of trouble. His mother snaps, calling him "Wild Thing!" and he yells right back, "I'll eat you up!"

Fed up, she sends him to his room to go to bed without any supper. But in his bedroom Max uses his imagination to escape into his own fantastic world.

When his mother calls him, "Wild Thing!" Max yells right back, "I'll eat you up!"

He has a wonderful time in the place where he meets the wild things, which are huge monsters he will tame. Suddenly, good smells reach him from

Maurice Sendak and all his "wild things."

home, making him homesick. Gladly, he returns to his room, where he finds a hot supper and a big piece of cake waiting for him.

Some people thought that *Where the Wild Things Are* had gone too far. They admitted that Sendak was an enormously talented illustrator, but they questioned whether his new book was right for children. Maybe the wild things made the book too scary and would cause nightmares.

Without even reading *Where the Wild Things Are*, a famous psychologist named Bruno Bettelheim said it was dangerous. In a column in *Ladies' Home Journal* magazine, he warned mothers against letting their children read the book because it might make them worry about being abandoned by their mothers. Still other grown-ups thought the book would cause bad behavior, because children would want to act like Max.

But Sendak also had many fans who loved the book. The year after it was published, librarians honored him with the Caldecott Medal, an annual award for the best illustrated children's book. Maurice Sendak appreciated the award.

Sendak is an enor—mously talented illustrator.

But what he liked even more was the praise he received from young readers. It delighted him that children loved *Where the Wild Things Are*. They related to Max getting in trouble and LIKED his adventures. To this day he treasures one letter from an eight-year-old boy who asked, "How much does it cost to get to where the wild things are? If it is not expensive, my sister and I would like to spend the summer there."

Chapter 2
Growing Up

Maurice Sendak was born on June 10, 1928, to Philip and Sarah Sendak, in Brooklyn, New York, one of five boroughs of New York City. A borough is a city that is part of a much larger city. New York City's most famous borough is Manhattan, and Brooklyn sits right across the East River from it. Manhattan has Wall Street, skyscrapers, and fancy hotels and department stores. People seem constantly in a hurry there. But Brooklyn is a very different place with quiet neighborhoods and tree-lined streets. The pace of life is much slower.

Maurice Sendak was born in Brooklyn, New York.

To many people, it seems a nice place to raise a family.

Maurice Sendak's parents were immigrants. They had both been born in Poland, a country in central Europe. They were both Jewish, too. Their shared background helped make for a strong marriage.

Philip Sendak, Maurice's father, liked to talk of his memories of life in Poland. Because Philip's father was a merchant who earned plenty of money, he was able to give his family a comfortable life. Philip had a happy childhood. One special memory was of skating on frozen ponds in the winter and coming in afterwards for hot drinks and sweet pastries.

He came to the United States as a young man because a young woman with whom he was in love immigrated. He did, in fact, find her in the United States. But they did not marry because she had already met someone else.

Sadie, as Maurice's mother was nicknamed, had different memories. Her

> **Maurice's parents had been born in Poland. They were Jewish, too.**

family was poor and lived in a tiny village where her father owned a grocery story. Sadie described her childhood as a sad and scary time. Jews were persecuted in her part of the country. Cossacks, who are soldiers on horseback, sometimes rode into their village, looking for Jews to imprison. When they came, she and her siblings ran, terrified, to hide in their cellar.

When Sadie was 15, her father died. Her mother sent Sadie to the United States to find work. The plan was that she would send money home so everyone else in the family could come to the United States, too.

Both of Maurice Sendak's parents were happy to have had the chance to come to America, which they regarded as a land of opportunity. Philip Sendak was a tailor. Sadie, like many women of the day, was a homemaker. Maurice was their third child. He had a sister, Natalie, who was nine when he was born. His brother Jack was five years older than he was.

Maurice's parents were glad to have the chance to come to the United States, which they regarded as the land of opportunity.

Maurice's father, Philip, was a great storyteller.

In 1929, a little more than a year after Maurice was born the United States entered the Depression. During this period, times were hard everywhere. There were few jobs and many families had to struggle to find food and other basic necessities.

Philip Sendak's business fell off during the Depression. The Sendak family, like many others, became poor. But they scraped their pennies together every Friday night so they could go to the movies. To this day, Maurice Sendak remembers watching *King Kong*, *Fantasia*, and Charlie Chaplin's funny films. He especially loved watching the Mickey Mouse cartoons that were shown between features.

Philip Sendak was a natural-born storyteller, so he filled his children's imaginations, too. Maurice Sendak remembers that "he would sit at the edge of the bed and tell us cliffhangers. Some of these I repeated in school and was sent home with instructions to have my mouth washed out. My father didn't censor himself or worry about what was appropriate for children. We idolized him."

As a boy, Sendak began to create his own stories. He wrote one of his first with his brother, Jack. It resembled a soap opera, revolving around a brother who has suffered a very bad accident. Realizing he will soon die, his sister jumps out of the window of the hospital with him, rather than endure life without him.

Beginning when he was a very small boy, Maurice was often sick. He came down with measles when he was two. It took him weeks to recover because he also developed double pneumonia. From that point on, his parents regarded him as delicate and frail.

When he was small, Maurice Sendak could not skate or play ball well. Rather than go out to play, he liked to stay inside and draw. Because he did not fit in well with other children, he didn't make very many friends. But he was

As a boy, Maurice began to make up his own stories.

part of a huge extended family. The Sendaks had many relatives who lived in and around New York City. They exchanged visits every Sunday, visiting each other's homes.

Every so often, the Sendak family moved to a new apartment. When Maurice was seven, they moved to a place on 69th Street. That was a happy time, during which Maurice did feel strong. He learned to like to play outside. The next move was to West Sixth Street. On their new block, Maurice became popular because he could tell great stories from the movies.

Maurice did not like school very much.

Sendak generally did not like school, where he felt like he was constantly being corrected by his teachers. What made things worse was that some of them criticized Walt Disney, one of his personal heroes.

In 1939, World War II began in Europe. In 1941, the United States joined the war, fighting on the side of England and France against Germany and Japan. World War II was a hard time for many

Americans, including the Sendaks. Natalie had become engaged to a soldier who was killed in the war.

Philip spent a lot of time and money trying to make arrangements to bring family members who still lived in war-torn Poland to the United States. But he did not succeed. Because they were Jews, they were put to death during the Holocaust by the Germans. Looking back, Maurice Sendak remembered that he felt that he was not supposed to have any fun or enjoy himself all through the war.

During World War II, the Sendaks lost a lot of family members who still lived in Poland.

Chapter 3
Drawing

Maurice's best subject in school was art.

Maurice Sendak began high school during World War II, but did not do well in most of his subjects. But he excelled in art. He really liked his art teacher, who encouraged his students to develop their own styles. Sendak drew a comic strip for his school newspaper. His drawings also appeared in a student magazine and the yearbook.

In his free time, he visited the Museum of Modern Art and the Metropolitan Museum of Art. After school, he worked at All-American Comics where he drew backgrounds for the Mutt and Jeff comic strip. His high school physics teacher was so impressed with Sendak's drawings that he helped him land a job making drawings for a textbook called *Atomics for the Millions*. The drawings he made for the book were eye-catching and funny.

Maurice Sendak finished high school in 1946. After graduation, he went to work for a company that put together window displays for department stores. In 1948, he quit his job after several of his friends were fired and he was out of work all summer. Depressed because he was out of money and had to move back home, he cheered himself up by sketching children he saw out his window. He also built toys with Jack and hoped to sell them in toy stores. Buyers at the famous F.A.O. Schwarz toy store said their inventions would be too expensive to manufacture.

But its window display director gave Sendak a job. At the store, he especially enjoyed time he spent in the children's book department. He became fascinated by children's books'

After he graduated from high school, Maurice went to work for a company that made window displays for stores.

illustrations. He found illustrators he considered geniuses, like George Cruikshank, Walter Crane, and Randolph Caldecott.

At night, he attended classes at an art school. He practiced his own drawing and began to dream of becoming an illustrator. When the book buyer at F.A.O. Schwarz found out he hoped one day to illustrate children's books, she introduced him to Ursula Nordstrom, an editor at Harper and Brothers publishing company.

Nordstrom looked at sketches Sendak had made at F.A.O. Schwarz. Soon she offered him a job doing the illustrations for a book called *The Wonderful Farm*, by Marcel Aymé. He had a happy time working on the book.

Nordstrom was so pleased with his work she asked him to do something else, the illustrations for *A Hole Is To Dig*. This was a book like no other of the time. The author, Ruth Krauss, had simply talked to children and written down their definitions of simple words.

At night, Maurice attended classes at an art school.

Her book did not tell a story, but listed definitions, like "Dogs are to kiss people" and "Hands are to hold." When Nordstrom showed the book to one illustrator, he refused to do it, saying there was nothing there.

But when she showed the manuscript to Sendak, he loved it. Krauss, Nordstrom, and Sendak were all very happy with the illustrations he came up with. They looked a lot like the pictures he had made of children playing on the streets of Brooklyn.

A Hole Is To Dig was a big hit and sold many copies. It made Sendak so much money that he was able to quit his job at the toy store and move out of his parents' house. He got an apartment in Greenwich Village and started working full-time as an illustrator.

By this time, Sendak had become very interested in what he thought made a good children's book. Nordstrom showed him many, many books, which they discussed. Krauss

He became fascinated with children's book illustrators.

shared her ideas with him, too. He started to collect books he loved.

After *A Hole Is To Dig*, Sendak worked on many other projects, including book covers and advertisements in addition to his illustrations. He started to work a great deal with two other authors, Meindert DeJong and Else Holmelund Minarik, who wrote the Little Bear books.

In 1953, he took his first trip to Europe where he learned a great deal about art in some of the finest museums in the world. When he came back home, he adopted a dog, a terrier he named Jennie. She became his best friend. A life-long bachelor, Sendak enjoyed having a pet to look after and care for.

At age 27, he took another new step. He wrote his first book, *Kenny's Window*. Looking back, he said it had too many words and described the illustrations as "ghastly." He felt much better about his next tries. His second book was about a small boy who becomes angry when his mother seems

"I never wrote a book where I told a lesson," says Sendak.

to spend all her time with a new baby. The third, *The Sign on Rosie's Door*, was about a little girl who cheers up her bored friends by helping them put on a show.

He and Nordstrom especially enjoyed working on what they titled *The Nutshell Library*, four tiny books that would come in a box. As he wrote, he developed his own style. Later he would say, "I never wrote a book where I taught a lesson." Instead, what he liked to do was to try to capture the feeling of what it is like to be a child in his books.

Maurice Sendak at his drawing table.

By the time he had illustrated dozens of books for other authors, Maurice wanted to write his own picture book.

Soon he had illustrated 50 books. Now he wanted to strike out and write a picture book, one with few words that depends on pictures to help tell the story.

For years, he had been thinking about writing a book about a child's escape into his imagination. So in 1963, he used his ideas to write and illustrate *Where the Wild Things Are*. Over the years it has become recognized as a classic and has been translated into more than a dozen languages. Millions of copies have been sold, making it one of the ten best-selling children's books of all time.

Chapter 4
Success
and Sadness

Where the Wild Things Are made
Maurice Sendak famous. He continued
to love his work. But he began to have
serious problems in his life. In the mid-
1960s, his mother became sick with
cancer. He worried about her a great
deal. Then, in 1967, he was in England.
In the middle of an interview, he
suddenly found himself unable to
speak. A doctor told him the next day
that he had suffered a serious heart
attack. He was then 38. He felt shocked
and scared.

He stayed in a nursing home in
England to rest and recuperate. He

**Where the
Wild Things
Are made
Maurice
Sendak
famous.**

In 1967, Maurice suffered a serious heart attack.

refused to tell his parents he was sick because of Sadie's cancer. He did not want to cause them any more worry. So he had a friend send them postcards from all over Europe, making them think he was still enjoying a long vacation.

Then he received even more bad news. When he went to Europe, he had left his dog, Jennie, behind in the care of a friend. Now he found out Jennie was sick. Ignoring his doctor's advice, Maurice Sendak flew back to the United States to be with Jennie. There he got better but she did not. He had to have her put to sleep. In less than a year, his mother also died.

This was a time of great sadness for Sendak. Yet his sadness inspired him to write two new books that can only be described as joyful. First came *Higglety Pigglety Pop!*, a story about an adventuresome dog, for which he drew many pictures of Jennie. Then he turned to a book he called *In the Night Kitchen*. He drew on his happy memories of spending time in the kitchen with his mother when he was a little boy to write this book. In many of its pictures, he included things from his childhood. *In the Night Kitchen* would always be one of his very favorite books. Some people did not like it, however. That book would be banned from many libraries because its hero, Mickey, appears bare on one page!

In 1970, Sendak became the first American illustrator ever to receive the Hans Christian Andersen Award. This is the most important award given to illustrators and receiving one has been described as being the equivalent of getting the Nobel Prize. In the years that followed, he

Sendak enjoys autographing his books for his adoring fans.

In 1979, Sendak designed the costumes and sets for Mozart's *Magic Flute*.

would continue to do beautiful illustrations for many more books.

He also started to do something entirely new. Maurice Sendak has always loved classical music, especially opera. He often writes or draws while listening to music. He dreamed of getting involved himself in opera. In the late 1970s, he got his chance when an orchestra conductor named Frank Corsaro asked him to help stage operas. In 1979, Sendak designed the costumes and sets for Mozart's *Magic Flute* when it was performed in Houston, Texas. He had a wonderful time inventing a smoke-belching dragon and hot-air balloon that were used in the opera.

Also in 1979, an international organization named UNESCO asked Corsaro and Sendak to make *Where the Wild Things Are* into an opera. Sendak wrote the libretto (or words) for the opera's songs. He also designed its sets and costumes. In 1981, Sendak and Corsaro worked on another opera, *The*

Cunning Little Vixen, which appeared in New York.

In 1983, he worked on what may be his masterpiece, *The Nutcracker* ballet for Pacific Northwest Ballet in Seattle, Washington. Looking back on the experience, Sendak remembered that when he was asked to do designs for it, his impulse was to refuse. *The Nutcracker* has been performed over and over again. He thought it would be too boring and predictable. He also thought it would be too big a job—he'd have to come up with 180 costumes, for one thing. But then he met Pacific Northwest Ballet's artistic director, Kent Stowell. He discovered that Stowell "wished me to join him in a leap into the unknown."

Sendak went back to the very beginning, which was a short story written by a German named E.T.A. Hoffman in 1816. Sendak found out most ballets are drawn from a variation of that story. Together he and Stowell went to work to stage a ballet that was

Sendak has always enjoyed opera.

Maurice Sendak (left) with Hillary Rodham Clinton reading to a group of preschool children.

more true to the original. They made Claire, the little girl who is given the nutcracker at a Christmas party, into a strong heroine. Their production received great praise. Sendak enjoyed working on it so much that afterwards he drew pictures for a new edition of the Hoffmann book.

Chapter 5
Today

Maurice Sendak is a very private individual. For years, he has lived alone. He shares his house only with his dogs.

As a child he had trouble making friends. As an adult, he has formed some deep friendships, although he does not usually spend a great deal of time with his friends, seeing them only from time to time. He has especially enjoyed his friendships with other authors and illustrators, notably Tomi Ungerer and James Marshall.

He has also kept in touch over the years with some of his students. He

Maurice Sendak is a very private individual.

once taught a course in children's literature at Yale for two years. He has also been a teacher at the Parsons School of Design, where he and book designer Jane Byers Bierhorst taught a seminar on picture book illustration for years. He says he tried not to influence his students' style, but just give them direction.

In his free time, he loves to read and collect books.

In his free time, Maurice Sendak loves to read. His friends say that he often becomes so enthusiastic about books that he inspires them to go out and buy whatever he's been praising. He still collects books, especially illustrated books for children. He watches TV, too. Interested in popular culture, he watches Saturday morning cartoons and soap operas as well as more educational programs. He will always continue to spend most of his time writing, drawing, and listening to music.

In 1996, he received a great honor when President Bill Clinton gave him the National Medal of the Arts on behalf of the National Endowment for the Arts. In the fall of 2000, an animated television program based on his *Seven Little Monsters* started to air on the PBS network as part of its *Bookworm Bunch* series. Clearly he remains one of the world's best-loved children's book authors and illustrators.

Selected Works by Maurice Sendak

Higglety Pigglety Pop! Or There Must Be More to Life (New York: Harper & Row, 1967).

In the Night Kitchen (New York: Harper & Row, 1970).

Kenny's Window (New York: Harper & Row, 1956).

The Nutshell Library (New York: Harper & Row, 1962). This set includes *Alligators All Around, Chicken Soup with Rice, One Was Johnny,* and *Pierre.*

Outside Over There (New York: Harper & Row, 1981).

Seven Little Monsters (New York: Harper & Row, 1976).

The Sign on Rosie's Door (New York: Harper & Row, 1960).

Very Far Away (New York: Harper & Row, 1957).

Where the Wild Things Are (New York: Harper & Row, 1963).

Maurice Sendak has also illustrated dozens of books written by other people. Some include:

DeJong, Meindert, *The Wheel on the School* (Harper & Row, 1954).

Hoffmann, E. T. A., *Nutcracker* (New York: Crown Publishers, 1984).

Joslin, Sesyle, *What Do You Say, Dear?* (New York: Young Scott, 1958).

Krauss, Ruth, *A Hole Is To Dig* (New York: Harper & Row, 1952).

Marshall, James, *Swine Lake* (New York: 1999).

Minarik, Else Holmelund, *Little Bear* (Harper & Row, 1957). Sendak would also illustrate the other three Little Bear books.

Zolotow, Charlotte, *Mr. Rabbit and the Lovely Present* (New York: Harper & Row, 1962).

He is one of the best-loved children's authors and illus— trators.

Chronology

- 1928, born on June 10, in Brooklyn, New York.
- 1946, graduates from high school.
- 1948, leaves his first job as a window-dresser and goes to work for F. A. O. Schwarz, a famous toy store.
- 1951, illustrates *A Hole Is To Dig*, a book by Ruth Krauss which earns him a reputation as a gifted illustrator.
- 1956, publishes the first book he writes and illustrates, *Kenny's Window*.
- 1963, publishes *Where the Wild Things Are*.
- 1964, is awarded the Caldecott Medal for his illustrations in *Where the Wild Things Are*.
- 1967, suffers a heart attack.
- 1968, both his mother and his beloved dog die.
- 1970, becomes first American illustrator to receive the Hans Christian Andersen Award.
- 1978, begins to design operas, working on their sets and costumes.
- 1983, designs *The Nutcracker* for Pacific Northwest Ballet in Seattle, Washington.
- 1988, makes publishing history when one of his books has a first print run of 250,000 copies, the largest ever for a children's book up to that point.
- 1996, receives the National Endowment of the Arts National Medal of the Arts.
- 1999, publishes *Swine Lake*, written by James Marshall. By now, Sendak has worked on more than 80 books in his long and distinguished career.

Index